Published by Evans Brothers Limited
2A Portman Mansions
Chiltern Street
London W1U 6NR

© Evans Brothers Limited 2006

Produced for Evans Brothers Limited by
White-Thomson Publishing Ltd,
Bridgewater Business Centre,
210 High Street,
Lewes, East Sussex BN7 2NH

Printed in China by New Era Printing Co. Ltd .

Project manager: Ruth Nason

Designer: Helen Nelson, Jet the Dog

Series consultant: Rosie-Turner Bisset, Reader in
Education and Director of Learning and Teaching,
Faculty of Education, University of Middlesex

British Library Cataloguing in Publication Data
Riley, Peter D.
    Rich and poor in Tudor times. - (Step-up history)
    1. Great Britain - Social conditions - 16th century
    - Juvenile literature
    2. Great Britain - History - Tudors, 1485-1603 -
    Juvenile literature
    I. Title
    942'.05

ISBN-13: 9780237531478
ISBN-10: 023753147X

Picture acknowledgements:

Bridgeman Art Library: pages 1/5t (Private
Collection), 4 (Private Collection), 7 (Rafael Valls
Gallery, London), 11 (Private Collection), 13
(Bibliotheque Nationale, Paris), 18b (Longleat
House, Wiltshire), 22 (Private Collection), 24b
(Private Collection); Camera Press: pages 10
(photograph by CASS), 27t (photograph by James
Veysey); Corbis: pages 5b (Graham Tim/Corbis
Sygma), 6 (Bettmann), 15t (Bettmann), 20 (Robert
Estall), 21b (Philippa Lewis; Edifice), 24t (Robert
Estall), 26 (Oskanen Tessa/Corbis Sygma); Getty
Images: pages 8t, 9, 12t, 14; Mary Evans Picture
Library: page 12b; National Trust Photo Library:
cover, left centre (Derrick E. Witty), pages 8b
(Matthew Antrobus), 16t (Rod J. Edwards), 16b and
cover top right (Derek Croucher), 17t (Andreas von
Einsiedel), 17b (Andreas von Einsiedel), 18t
(Andreas von Einsiedel), 19 (Chris King), 21t (Erik
Pelham); Topfoto: pages 23 and cover top left
(Topham/Fotomas), 27b (TopFoto.co.uk).

Contents

Tudor times

Find today on the timeline below. You can see that a little more than 100 years ago the reign of Queen Victoria came to an end. Also the first aeroplane flew. If you go back another 100 years, you will find that George III was king. During his reign the first steam locomotive was built.

About 300 years ago Queen Anne was the monarch. Daily newspapers were beginning to be produced. Just over 400 years before now you find the end of the reign of Elizabeth I. She was the last of the Tudor monarchs.

Plenty of evidence

Tudor times are not long ago compared to Viking and Anglo-Saxon times, which ended nearly 1,000 years ago, and Roman times, which ended 1,600 years ago. This means that many things from Tudor times, such as cloth

▲ *The years from 1485 to 1603 are known as Tudor times because the kings and queens of England in that time were from the Tudor family. In this picture, what tells you that Elizabeth I and the* courtiers *around her are rich?*

and objects made from wood, have survived. Tudor buildings, tombs, paintings, drawings and written documents still exist. Historians and archaeologists can use all this evidence to learn about the lives of Tudor people.

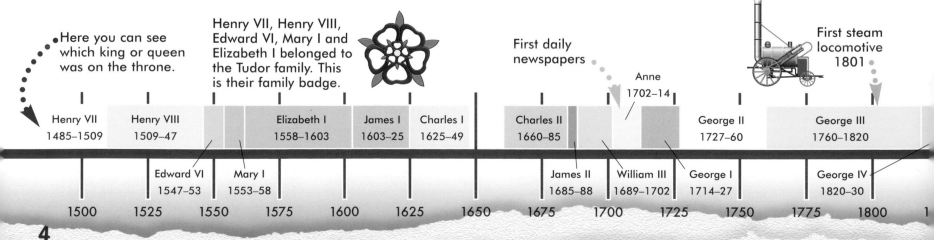

Here you can see which king or queen was on the throne.

Henry VII, Henry VIII, Edward VI, Mary I and Elizabeth I belonged to the Tudor family. This is their family badge.

First daily newspapers

First steam locomotive 1801

| Henry VII 1485–1509 | Henry VIII 1509–47 | | Elizabeth I 1558–1603 | James I 1603–25 | Charles I 1625–49 | | Charles II 1660–85 | | Anne 1702–14 | | George II 1727–60 | | George III 1760–1820 |

Edward VI 1547–53 — Mary I 1553–58 — James II 1685–88 — William III 1689–1702 — George I 1714–27 — George IV 1820–30

1500 1525 1550 1575 1600 1625 1650 1675 1700 1725 1750 1775 1800

Busy times

Tudor times were eventful. Henry VIII built up the English navy but destroyed the monasteries. Elizabeth I defended England against a Spanish invasion by defeating a fleet of ships called the Armada. She also encouraged sailors to make voyages of discovery.

The people

There were three million people in England when Tudor times began and this grew steadily to five million by the end. A few, the rich, could enjoy everything that their world could offer – fine clothes, large houses, great feasts. Most people lived all their lives in the same village, working together, enjoying pastimes together, worshipping in the church together and then being buried in the same churchyard.

In Tudor times it was possible for a villager to gather wealth and become rich. It was also possible to lose everything and become poor. In time there were so many poor people that the monarch and the rich had to help them.

▲ *This drawing from 1569 shows a rich man walking past a beggar.*

▼ *Today, soldiers called the Yeomen of the Guard take part in formal occasions where the Queen, Elizabeth II, is present. Their uniform was designed in Tudor times, for the bodyguard of Henry VII.*

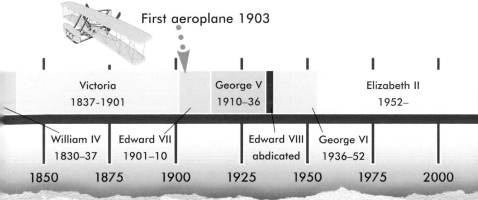

First aeroplane 1903

		Victoria 1837–1901		George V 1910–36			Elizabeth II 1952–	
	William IV 1830–37	Edward VII 1901–10			Edward VIII abdicated	George VI 1936–52		
1850	1875	1900	1925	1950	1975	2000		

Landowners

Long before the Tudors, monarchs rewarded their courtiers by giving them huge areas of land – often thousands of acres. Courtiers were also given titles, such as Earl or Lord. When a courtier died, his lands and title passed to one of his descendants.

Many landowners in Tudor times were either courtiers of the Tudor monarch or the descendants of courtiers from earlier times. They were known as the nobility. Other landowners, who were not courtiers or nobles, were known as the gentry. They included merchants who had become wealthy through trade. When Henry VIII closed the monasteries, he sold their land to people like this.

Growing rich from the land

Landowners built themselves splendid houses on their land, which showed their wealth and power. They did not work on the land themselves. This was done by farm workers who rented the land. The landowner had two officials, called the bailiff and the steward, who supervised the work of the farmers and collected the rent from them. The landowners grew rich from the rents they were paid.

▲ Landowners had a great deal of leisure time. They built tennis courts, mazes and bowling alleys by their houses to amuse themselves and their guests. They also hunted deer with dogs and birds with hawks. This picture from a book about hunting showed how to entertain an important guest at a hunting party.

The clothes of the rich

The nobility and gentry dressed in fine clothes, showing that they did not need to work. The materials used were silk, satin, velvet and fur.

Men wore a tight-fitting jacket, called a doublet, and hose (similar to tights). It was fashionable for the hose to be stuffed with cloth or horse hair from the knee to the waist, to make them bulge out.

Women wore a farthingale under their skirt to make the skirt spread out around them when they stood or walked. It became fashionable for men and women to wear a ruff around their neck. People liked to show their wealth by the most expensive jewellery they could afford.

Rich children

The children of the rich were dressed in gowns until the age of six. Then they wore the same clothes as the adults. Rich parents bought their children toys from France and Holland. Girls received wooden dolls, which had painted faces and limbs with movable joints. Boys were given soldiers and drums. Both boys and girls played with hoops.

Rich children had tutors who lived in their homes. They learned languages such as French, Italian and Latin. They also learned to sing, dance, play musical instruments and to ride a horse. The purpose of this education was to prepare them to enter the monarch's court and become a courtier.

Make a ruff

Fold a paper doyley (24 cm in diameter) in half and cut away the centre. Make one cut from the edge to the centre so you can put on the 'ruff' over your collar. A real ruff was made of stiff cloth. Do you think it was comfortable to wear?

▶ *How old would you say these Tudor children are? Compare their clothes with what children wear today.*

Merchants

Making money

There was a great increase in trade in Tudor times and some merchants made a lot of money. For example, a merchant would buy woollen cloth from weavers in England. He would take the cloth to France and trade or exchange it, with French merchants, for silk material. Back in England, he would sell the silk for more money than the price he had paid for the woollen cloth. Merchants sold the silk either to townspeople or to tailors, who would make it into clothes.

The merchant could use some of the money he made to buy more wool. He traded this wool for more silk and made even more money when he sold the silk. In time he made enough money to buy a large house in a town, or land and a mansion in the countryside. Successful merchants became part of the gentry.

▶ *This house in Coggeshall, Essex, was built by a wealthy wool merchant called John Paycocke.*

▲ *A merchant stored his goods in a warehouse before they were sold or traded. The merchant is on the left in this picture. What is he doing? What are his workmen doing?*

As a merchant became more successful, he dressed himself and his family in finer clothes. He copied the ways of the nobility, having portraits painted of himself and his family.

Grammar schools

From about the twelfth century, monasteries ran schools, called grammar schools, where children could learn to read and write in Latin and Greek. These were the languages used for writing books. When Henry VIII closed the monasteries, in 1535-41, most of the schools were shut down. Later, in Edward VI's reign, new grammar schools were paid for by craft guilds (see page 11) and by some very wealthy merchants. The children of merchants, traders and yeoman farmers attended these schools.

Boys and girls entered a grammar school at the age of six or seven. They learnt to read and write in English, Latin and Greek. The girls left after a few years to help in the home. The boys stayed on until the age of 15 or 16, when they could go to a university if they wished. At university a young man could learn how to become a doctor or a lawyer. These professions could make people wealthy.

Louth Grammar School was founded in 1552. The school seal shows scholars at work and a schoolmaster punishing one of them for unsatisfactory work.

Tudor money

Merchants traded a certain amount of their goods for other goods, but they also sold their goods for money. Money was counted in pounds (£), shillings (s) and pennies (d). Twelve pennies were equal to the value of one shilling and 20 shillings were equal to the value of £1. If something had a value of 15 pennies, for example, its price would be written as 1s 3d. If it had a value of 35 shillings, its price would be written as £1 15s.

Can you work it out?

Can you calculate with Tudor money? What would be the prices of something with a value of (a) 26 pennies, (b) 51 shillings. If you added 6s 7d to 3s 8d, how much money would you have in shillings and pennies?

Craftsmen and traders

A group of people who were neither rich nor poor were the master craftsmen. They included people who made things, such as a carpenter making chairs, and people who processed food, such as a butcher cutting up meat. They were also traders. They sold their goods to people in their town and to merchants. They did not deal with other traders in other countries, as many rich merchants did.

Growing towns

Many of the first towns in England grew up around monasteries. The people lived there to supply food and goods to the monks. In Tudor times these towns expanded as master craftsmen supplied goods for merchants to trade.

Other towns grew from villages that were close to large roads or rivers. The roads and rivers allowed goods for trade to be transported easily.

Traders in towns

If you walked through a Tudor town, you would discover that all the butchers' shops were together in one street. Other traders, such as bakers, fishmongers and goldsmiths, were also grouped in separate streets. Street names like Bread Street and Goldsmiths Row often showed who was trading there.

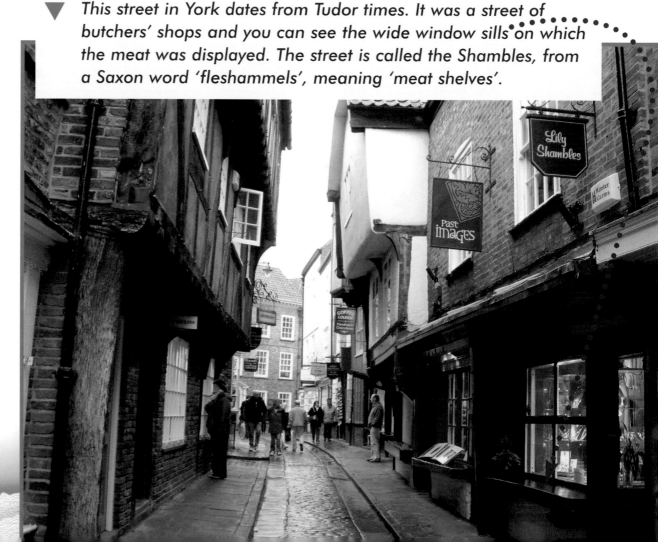

▼ *This street in York dates from Tudor times. It was a street of butchers' shops and you can see the wide window sills on which the meat was displayed. The street is called the Shambles, from a Saxon word 'fleshammels', meaning 'meat shelves'.*

Craft guilds

Each master craftsman was a member of a craft guild, such as the bakers' guild and the shoe-makers' guild. To become a master craftsman, you had to serve as an apprentice to another master for two to seven years. Then you became a journeyman, employed by a master. A journeyman could become a master if his work was of a very high standard and he could pay money to join the guild.

Once someone became a master, he had to take on apprentices. This ensured that the guild would survive. The money paid into the guild was used to help masters who were ill. Also, when a master died, the guild provided money for his widow and children so that they would not become poor.

Craftsmen's children

Masters' children could become apprentices when they were seven or eight. One of the guild rules was that children could not stay to learn a trade from their father. They had to go to live at another master's house.

Most trades took in boys to serve as apprentices but some, such as butchers, bookbinders and goldsmiths, took in girls too. The guilds of the spinners and silk makers only took in girls.

Coats of arms

The craft guilds of London are also known as the City Livery Companies. Go to http://www.wcsim.co.uk/page04.htm and look at the coats of arms of the following companies: (25) saddlers, (26) carpenters, (38) bowyers. What can you see on their coats of arms which might indicate the work of the members?

▼ These pictures are from the rule book for the bakers' guild in York.

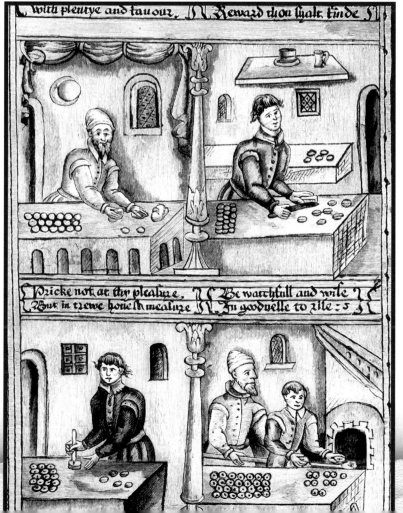

11

Farming the land

At the beginning of Tudor times most people in England lived in a village and farmed the land around it, which they rented from the landowner. There were large open fields, without hedges or walls, where the villagers grew crops. Beyond the fields was pasture, where the villagers grazed their cattle. There were also woodlands, where pigs could forage and villagers collected wood for fuel.

Harvesting, 1577. There was work to do in the fields for most of the year. In winter the men worked on repairing roads.

Three types of farmers

A few farmers saved enough money to buy the land they farmed from the owner. They were known as yeoman farmers. They had more money than other villagers but were not rich enough to join the gentry.

Many farmers, called tenant farmers, rented enough land to produce more food than they needed. They sold their surplus food to townspeople, who had no land to grow or produce their own. Tenant farmers were not poor, but they had much less money than yeoman farmers.

This woman is walking to town to sell the eggs in her basket.

Some villagers could only afford a small rent and had a small patch in a field to grow corn. They could keep only one cow and one pig. They were called tenants-at-will. They could not produce enough food for themselves and so they had to work for others as well as working on their own land. They were poor.

Country clothes

Village people could not afford the fine clothes of the rich. They wore clothes that helped them do their work and kept them warm. Women wore a long-sleeved long dress, an apron and leather shoes. Men wore a tunic, trousers and hobnailed boots.

▼ *Anthony Fitzherbert's 'Boke of Husbandry' (Book of Farming), published in 1523, gave this advice about what a farmer's wife should do each morning.*

Set all good things in order within thy house: milk thy kye, suckle thy calves, syc up thy milk, take up thy children and array them and provide for thy husband's breakfast, dinner and supper and for thy children and servants, and take thy part with them. And to ordain corn and malt to the mill, to bake and brew withal when need is.

Words you need to know: thy = your
kye = cow   syc up = filter out solids from
array = dress   ordain = send
withal = with them

Farmers' children

The countryside was divided into areas of land called parishes. In each parish there was a church and at least one village. The priest at the church ran a school for all the children in the parish. Children spent most of their time helping the adults farm their land, but they went to the parish school for up to two years to learn to read and write. They did not attend the school regularly, because at many times of year they were needed to sow corn, scare birds or harvest the crops.

Could you be a bird scarer?

A bird scarer stood in a field for hours and stopped birds from feeding on newly sown seed and young crops. Look out of a window over a garden or school field. Stay there for ten minutes and record how many birds you see to scare away. How do you think Tudor children felt, spending hours in a field to scare birds?

◄ *When villagers had time for leisure they enjoyed dancing.*

The poorest people

Driven off the land

A change in farming led to an increase in poverty in Tudor times. Trade developed between England and other countries and one of the trade goods that was in great demand was wool. Landowners discovered that they could make more money by raising sheep on their land, to produce wool, than they could by renting the land to farmers. The landowners wanted to clear the farmers off their land, so they evicted tenant farmers and tenants-at-will when their rent agreements came to an end.

Farming sheep needed many fewer people than sowing and harvesting crops. Each flock needed only a shepherd. So, when landowners changed to sheep farming, farmers and their families lost their jobs as well as their land.

Some yeoman farmers continued to grow crops and some evicted farmers went to work for them. Others had to look for work elsewhere. They moved around the countryside looking for casual work, such as tending the gardens of great houses, or they went to towns to look for work as labourers or servants to merchants and craftsmen.

Does this picture from 1579 give the impression that the shepherd is poor?

Closing the monasteries

After Henry VIII closed the monasteries, the monks tried to find work in grammar schools. People who had lived around the monastery and worked for the monks as stonemasons and carpenters lost their homes and their work. They became very poor.

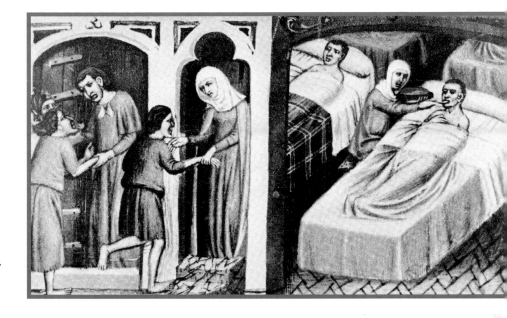

▶ *Monasteries gave food and shelter to the poor and sick. This source of help was lost when the monasteries were closed.*

Three groups of poor people

The government divided the poor into three groups:

- the helpless poor or deserving poor. They were not capable of having a job. They included orphan children and people who were incurably ill, such as the blind, the lame and lepers.
- the able-bodied poor. They were well enough to work, and wanted to work, but could not find a job.
- rogues and vagabonds. They could work but chose not to. They roamed the countryside, often in gangs, visiting villages and towns where they stole money or property.

On page 24 you will learn how the government made laws to deal with these groups.

Vagabond talk

Vagabonds had their own words, so they could talk to each other without others understanding. E.g.:
coneys = people to rob
drawing = picking pockets
lifts = stolen goods
boozing ken = an inn
peck = food.

What did this mean?
'Lots of coneys in the market for drawing. Bring your lifts to the boozing ken and we'll get some peck.'

◀ *Poverty and having no work drove many people to beg.*

Great houses

You can probably guess that both the houses on this page were built for wealthy landowners. What differences do you notice between them? The first one was built at the beginning of Tudor times. It is like a castle, with a tower, small windows, and a moat around it. Castles were built to protect people from attack in times of war.

Under the Tudor monarchs, life in England was more peaceful than in the past and the nobles realised that they no longer needed the protection of a castle. New homes, called great houses, were designed for comfort and to show off their owners' wealth. They were built from the most expensive materials – brick and carved stone. Large windows were another sign of wealth, as glass was very expensive in Tudor times.

▲ *Oxburgh Hall, Norfolk, was built at the end of the fifteenth century.*

▶ *Hardwick Hall was built in 1591-97, for Bess of Hardwick. She was a servant who married several rich men and became the richest woman in England, apart from the queen.*

House designs

The foundations of some great houses were laid out in the shape of the first letter of the monarch's name – for example, H for Henry and E for Elizabeth. Other houses were planned in the shape of a square, which was similar to the foundations of a castle. When the house was built it did not have battlements at the top but carved figures and balustrades.

▲ *This room at Hardwick Hall, called the long gallery, is 49 metres long. Long galleries became popular in sixteenth-century great houses, as somewhere to walk for exercise.*

▼ *This carved stone fireplace at Baddesley Clinton manor house dates from the 1530s.*

Visit Ingatestone Hall

Many rooms were needed for guests, servants and for the owner and his family. Look at the ground-floor and first-floor plans of Ingatestone Hall, at http://renaissance.dm.net/compendium/map-ingatestone.html.

What were the ground-floor rooms used for? What was different about the use of the first-floor rooms?

Interior decoration

The owner of the house decorated the inside to show his wealth. The walls were covered in wood panels to decorate them and keep the rooms warm. Wide staircases with carved stone or wood banisters were made between the floors. Carvings were a feature around doors too, and over the main fireplace there would be a carving of the family coat of arms.

Visiting a great house

Tudor great houses were also known as prodigy houses. Prodigy means marvellous. Imagine visiting one in Tudor times.

Your arrival

If you were rich you might be invited as a guest to a great house. You would probably arrive on a horse or in a carriage. You would be greeted at the main door by a servant and shown into the entrance hall. In front of you would be a large staircase, which you would climb to the first floor. This was where the owner lived and guests stayed.

▲ An important part of the senior servants' work was to carry food in a kind of procession up the grand staircase to the great chamber.

Mealtime

If it was time for a meal you would be shown into the great chamber. This was considered the most important room in the house and was where feasts took place. Here you would greet the owner, his family and other guests and dine with them. The main meal, called dinner, was eaten between 11 and 3 o'clock. Supper was smaller, eaten at about 5 o'clock.

▶ William Brooke, 10th Lord Cobham, and his family, in 1567. Tudors did not have forks. They used a knife and their fingers to eat.

After the meal

After the evening meal, if you were a close friend of the owner, you would be invited to join him and his family in the withdrawing chamber. Here you would chat or perhaps play a game such as cards.

If you were not a close friend, you would join other guests in the long gallery to listen to musicians play recorders, a lute and a viol. Perhaps you would join in a dance. Later, you would retire to your bedroom. Servants would have prepared your bed with clean blankets, made a fire in the fireplace and left flowers and herbs to give the room a pleasant smell.

Solve a Tudor riddle

Tudor children loved riddles. If you visited a great house, perhaps the owner would give you this riddle to solve. Try to explain what is going on.

Two legs sat upon three legs,
With one leg in his lap;
In comes four legs
And runs away with one leg;
Up jumps two legs,
Catches up three legs,
Throws it after four legs,
And makes him bring back one leg.

▶ *You may be able to visit a Tudor house today. These children are in the great chamber at Sutton House, London, built in 1535 by a courtier of Henry VIII.*

The work of a servant

If you belonged to the family of a farmer who had lost his land, you could get a job as a servant at a great house. You would be treated very differently from a rich guest. You would enter the house by a small door at the back. If a meal was in preparation, you might be set to work bringing food out of the larder into the kitchen. Then you might help bring wine from the cellar. Servants called grooms would carry the food to the great chamber and they would bring back dirty dishes and plates for you to wash in the scullery.

Afterwards you may be given leftover food from the great chamber. Then you would be set to work making candles. Finally, you would climb two flights of stairs to the second floor, to sleep in a small cold room.

Timber-framed houses

Houses like the ones on the left of the picture below are called timber-framed, or half-timbered, houses. Many were built in England in Tudor times for people who were quite wealthy but not rich, such as master craftsmen, yeoman farmers and some merchants.

The houses were built on stone foundations. Large pieces of timber were joined together to make a frame, to support the whole building. The gaps between the timbers were filled with hazel twigs, which were covered in mud or clay. The twigs were called wattle and the mud or clay was called daub. Often the wattle-and-daub walls were painted white.

Sometimes bricks were used instead of wattle and daub. The roof was made of thatch or tiles. The floors were covered with stone or wood.

The timbers were left exposed to the weather and became silvery brown. People who lived at various times after the Tudors covered the timbers with black paint or tar.

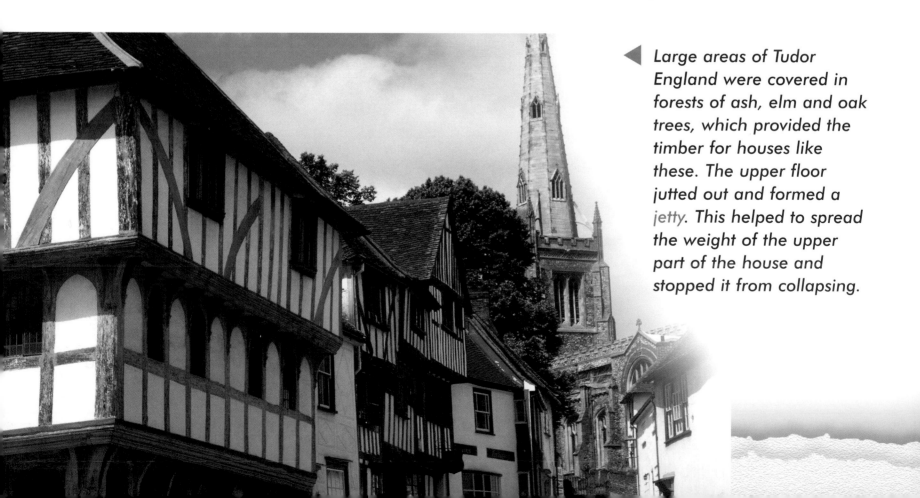

Large areas of Tudor England were covered in forests of ash, elm and oak trees, which provided the timber for houses like these. The upper floor jutted out and formed a *jetty*. This helped to spread the weight of the upper part of the house and stopped it from collapsing.

◄ *Inside a Tudor merchant's house in Tenby. A cauldron hangs in the fireplace, for cooking.*

House contents

People who lived in timber-framed houses had enough money to buy beds, chairs, high-backed benches called settles, cupboards and chests. The contents of the house were so important that people bequeathed them in their wills. When a person died, a list was made of all their possessions, with their value. The list was called an inventory. It was used with the will to help share out the goods to the relatives and friends of the dead person.

Fireplace and chimney

The fireplace and chimney were a major feature of the house. They were made of brick or stone, which would not burn and kept the fire safely away from the wooden frame.

A chimney draws air over a fire better than a hole in the roof (see page 22). Having a chimney meant that the fire could be made with coal, which needs a good supply of air to burn well. Burning coal produces more heat than burning wood so the change to burning coal made the houses warmer.

► *Tall chimneys like these are a sign that a house was built in the sixteenth century.*

► *Part of an inventory of a farmer who died in 1596. Inventories were usually very long.*

Bedsted with beddynge	xxxv s x d
Candelstykes	vi s ix d
Pewter cuppes	iii s x d
Settle	xv s vi d
Poetts and panes	ii s iv d
Fower lames	v s
Three shepe	xii s vi d
Bakon and beyffe	ii s x d

Identify the items

Tudors could spell words how they liked and sometimes used Roman numerals. Remember that, in prices, s is for shillings and d is for pennies. Try to identify the items in the inventory above. Work out the total value of all the items.

Homes of the poor

This sixteenth-century woodcut gives an idea of what poor people's homes were like. The skeleton represents Death, taking away a child.

Poor people lived in huts made from any materials that could be gathered easily, such as branches, stones and mud. Walls were made of stone or wattle and daub and the roof was made of thatch. Buildings like this have not survived. They were cleared away at later points in history and replaced with new houses. But we know about them from pictures and from Tudor people who wrote about them.

One room

There was only one room in the home. The floor was made of dry earth and was covered with straw. There was a hearth for a fire in the centre and a smoke hole in the roof above it. Smoke from the fire swirled around under the roof before escaping through the hole.

The simplest homes had only a door and no windows. Light came from the open door and from the fire. If a home had windows, they did not have glass. It was too expensive. A window might be simply a hole with a shutter to close it.

▲ *The fire was used for cooking. The main meal of the day, cooked in a cauldron, was a thin vegetable soup called broth, eaten with a little bread. The very poor could not afford meat, but if a rabbit was caught, its meat was added to the broth.*

Some windows were filled with a thin sheet of horn or parchment, which let in some light and kept out the wind and rain.

Furniture

The poor could not afford 'joined-up' furniture, like the pieces owned by richer people (see page 21). For mealtimes they made a table and bench from trestles and planks. They took this furniture to bits again to make room for the straw mattresses that they rolled out to sleep on.

Disease and death

Poor homes were colder, damper and draughtier than timber-framed houses. This made the inhabitants more likely to suffer from disease. Children caught diseases more easily than adults, just as they do today, but the children of the very poor did not have a good diet or enough food to help them get better. Many died.

One disease which attacked the rich and poor alike was the plague. A person became infected if they were bitten by a rat flea. Poor homes were built close together and the rubbish from the houses was simply left around them. This attracted large numbers of rats and increased the chances of the poor being infected.

▲ Sixteenth-century homes did not have toilets or running water. What can you learn from this picture about what people did with their waste?

Ring o' roses

When a person got the plague, a rash appeared as red circles on their skin and they began to sneeze. Most people who caught the disease died in three days.

Tudor people thought that the plague was carried by bad smells in the air. They carried a bunch of herbs and flowers, called a posy, believing that the sweet smell of the plants would protect them.

It is claimed that 'Ring a ring o' roses' describes the plague. Use the information here to explain what each line may refer to.

Ring a ring o' roses,
A pocket full of posies,
Atishoo! Atishoo!
We all fall down.

Helping the poor

Remember the differences between these three groups of poor people, described on page 15:

- the helpless poor or deserving poor
- the able-bodied poor
- rogues and vagabonds.

The number of poor people grew in Tudor times and, from the mid-sixteenth century, the monasteries were no longer there to help them. The government made laws about how the poor should be treated.

They considered that all the poor should stay in their own parish and that the people of the parish should give money, called alms, to look after them. Some of the money was used to build almshouses for the deserving poor. The money was also used to build workhouses. Here the able-bodied poor were given food and shelter in return for doing work such as weaving cloth or repairing roads in the parish.

As rogues and vagabonds wandered around the country committing crimes, the Poor Laws stated how they should be punished. In the

▲ *The tall chimneys of these four Tudor almshouses show that the houses had brick fireplaces in which coal could be burnt.*

Poor Laws these people were called vagrants – homeless people who roam from place to place.

There was no police force in Tudor times. A Justice of the Peace, helped by volunteers in the parish, made sure that the laws were carried out.

▶ *Punishments for vagrants included time in the stocks. What do you think people did when they saw someone in the stocks?*

The Poor Laws

1495 The deserving poor may beg in their own parish. Vagrants must be put in the stocks for three days.

1531 The deserving poor need a licence from a Justice of the Peace to beg in their own parish. Vagrants must be whipped.

1536 People in the parish should give money to officials of the church, who will give it to the deserving poor. Vagrants must be made to do work, such as repairing roads in the parish.

1547 The people of the parish must find somewhere for the deserving poor to live. In church, a collection for the poor must be made, but people may choose not to give any money. Vagrants can be made into slaves.

1549 The part of the laws about slaves was cancelled because it was thought too harsh.

1552 Licensed beggars must not sit outside to beg. They should call on people in the parish to beg.

1563 People who do not give to the collection in church must explain why not to the Justice of the Peace. If their explanation is not satisfactory, they may be sent to jail. Only the deserving poor who are disabled can call on people to beg. Other deserving poor must get alms from the parish.

1572 The first time vagrants over 14 years of age are caught, they must be whipped and a hole must be made in their right ear. If caught again, they can be put in prison or hung.

1576 Vagrants must be forced to live and work in a house of correction.

1597 Each parish must have an official called an overseer who looks after the poor. People in the parish must pay an amount of money called the poor rate, to be given to the poor. Vagrants must be whipped and sent back to the county where they last lived. Vagrants who keep being caught must be sent to work in the colonies.

▶ *Some rogues and vagabonds pretended to be ill and disabled, so that they could beg. This picture shows a 'soap eater'. Soap eaters used soap to make them look as if they had an illness with frothing of the mouth.*

Did the laws work?

Look at the Poor Laws above and decide if they made the people in the parish keen to help the poor. Did they stop poor people becoming vagrants?

Life in Tudor times

In Tudor England there was a small number of rich people and a large number of poor people. Think about the differences between the lives of the rich and the lives of the poor.

Tudor homes

If you were rich, you had a large home. Everyone in the family could have a separate bedroom and there were rooms for servants too. Some rich courtiers had two homes – one in London, where the monarch lived, and one in the country, on the land that they owned.

If you were poor, your home had only one room, in which your family cooked, ate and slept. There were no servants.

Tudor food

The meals of the rich included a large amount of meat. Rich people considered that vegetables were the food of the poor. If you were very rich in late Tudor times you may have eaten potatoes and sugar. These two foods began to be imported into England from other parts of the world.

Rich people ate enough food to keep them healthy. Poor people could only afford cheap food, such as vegetables and bread. They made the vegetables into a broth. Many poor people did not have enough food to stay healthy.

Then and now

As well as thinking of differences between the rich and the poor in Tudor times, try comparing life in Tudor times with life today. What differences and what similarities can you think of?

▶ *Do you think this modern photograph is similar to any Tudor picture in this book?*

Tudor clothes

Rich Tudors had many clothes made from the finest materials. If the style of clothes worn at court changed, they could afford to buy new clothes to stay in fashion. Poor people could afford only one set of clothes which they wore every day. They could not keep up with fashion.

Tudor pastimes

Rich children had well-made toys such as hoops, balls, carved and painted ships, and dolls with movable limbs and plenty of clothes. They also had books, musical instruments and playing cards and went riding or hunting with their parents. Poor children often had little time for play and had to work to earn money for the family. If they had enough money, they could buy poorly made toys from peddlers.

Many of the poor people in towns enjoyed bull-baiting and bear-baiting where the unfortunate animals were attacked with dogs. They also enjoyed cockfighting where two birds fought to the death.

Both rich and poor Tudors enjoyed plays and visited the theatre regularly. The poor people stood in front of the stage and the rich people sat in balconies around them.

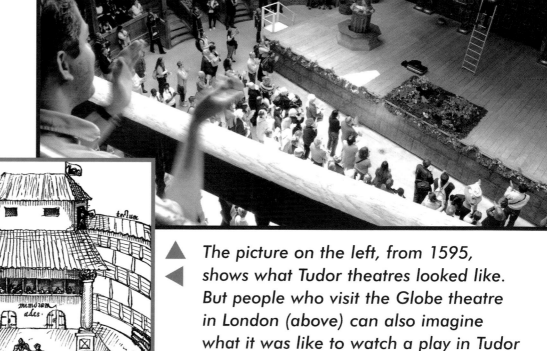

The picture on the left, from 1595, shows what Tudor theatres looked like. But people who visit the Globe theatre in London (above) can also imagine what it was like to watch a play in Tudor times. The Globe is a copy of a theatre that was there in the time of Elizabeth I.

Glossary

alms   money or food given to the poor.

apprentice   a person who is learning a trade and is supervised by a master.

archaeologists   people who study history by excavating sites inhabited in the past.

bailiff   a man who collected rents for a landowner.

baiting   tormenting an animal.

balustrade   a railing supported by short stone posts on the roof of a large building.

battlement   a wall on a roof, behind which soldiers could hide in an attack.

bequeath   to leave a possession to another person in a will.

carriage   a wheeled vehicle, pulled by horses, for transporting people.

cauldron   a large round pot for cooking liquids.

cellar   a room below ground, used to store goods such as wine.

chamber   a large room in a large house.

coat of arms   a symbol owned by a family or an organisation. The symbol, with a shield in the centre and surrounding features, was granted by a monarch.

colonies   areas of a country that have been settled by people from another country.

courtier   a member of the court, the group of people who attend meetings with the king or queen.

craft guild   an organisation for a group of craftsmen, which helps them carry out their work and supports them with money.

descendant   a person who is directly related to someone who was born before them. E.g. a child, grandchild, etc.

doublet   a short jacket with or without sleeves, which fits tightly to a man's body.

evict   to remove from a place, by force if necessary.

farthingale   a petticoat stiffened with hoops.

forage   to search for food.

gentry   a group of wealthy people, who did not help the monarch run the country.

grammar school   a school that taught Latin grammar.

groom   a male servant at a great house. Grooms were employed for many tasks. Some looked after the horses.

hawk   a small bird of prey.

hearth   the part of the floor where a fire is built.

hobnailed boots   boots with large-headed nails driven into their soles, to give good grip.

horn   a material made from cattle horns.

house of correction   a jail.

jetty   the overhanging part of an upper floor in a timber-framed house.

journeyman   a person who has reached a level of skill and knowledge where they no longer need a master's supervision. The word comes from the French 'journée' (day). A journeyman was paid daily for his work.

Justice of the Peace   an official of the government who makes sure that people obey the laws or receive punishments if they do not.

lame	unable to walk properly, because of a damaged foot or leg.	**profession**	a job for which someone must learn a great deal and gain complicated skills.
larder	a room for storing food.	**rent**	to make a payment, called rent, to a landowner for the use of his/her land.
leper	someone with leprosy, a disease that damages the skin and nerves.	**rogue**	a mischievous and dishonest person.
licence	a document giving permission to do something (e.g. to beg).	**ruff**	a white frill worn around the neck.
mansion	a very large house with many rooms.	**scullery**	a room for washing dishes.
master	a person with great knowledge and skills in a trade, who can teach others.	**seal**	a design stamped on a document to show where the document was made.
merchant	a person who trades or sells goods and may do business with merchants in other countries.	**settle**	a bench with arms and a high back, often placed near a fire.
moat	a deep ditch around a castle, sometimes filled with water.	**steward**	a man who supervised farming and other activities on a landowner's land.
monarch	a king or queen.	**stocks**	a device for punishment which held a wrongdoer so that people could mock or throw objects at them.
monastery	a place where monks live and worship.	**tailor**	a person who makes men's clothes.
monk	men who live under strict religious rules, such as taking part in acts of worship several times a day.	**tenant farmers**	farmers with documents from a court to show that they were entitled to farm a piece of land they did not own.
navy	the whole group of ships and their crews that a country has for protecting itself or attacking other countries.	**tenants-at-will**	farmers with no documents (see above).
nobility	a group of people who helped the monarch rule the country.	**trestle**	a framework of wood used to support a board to make a table.
orphan	a child whose parents have died.	**tutor**	a private teacher.
parchment	a thin sheet of material made from the skin of a sheep, goat or other animal.	**vagabond**	someone who wanders from place to place and may also be mischievous.
parish	a local area around a church. It may include a village or a part or the whole of a town.	**vagrant**	a homeless person who wanders about.
pasture	grassland for farm animals.	**will**	a document containing a person's instructions for who will receive their money and possessions after they die.
peddler	a person with a stock of small items, such as ribbons or toys, who travels around to sell them.	**workhouse**	a building in which the able-bodied poor lived and worked.
		yeoman farmer	a farmer who owns land but is not a member of the nobility or gentry.

For teachers and parents

This book is designed to support and extend the learning objectives for unit 8 of the QCA History Scheme of Work.

Most people know a little about the Tudors, in terms of the monarchs and the changes that took place in religion in Tudor times. Although this book focuses on the lives of 'ordinary' Tudor people, it is important to remember that those people were influenced by the monarchs (who had much more power than the monarch today) and by the consequences of the monarchs' actions. As a brief reminder, the Tudor monarchs and the dates of their reigns were: Henry VII (1485–1509), Henry VIII (1509–47), Edward VI (1547–53), Mary I (1553–58), Elizabeth I (1558–1603). The monasteries were closed during the reign of Henry VIII, and this had a large impact on swelling the ranks of the poor and reducing a source of care for them.

Before Tudor times there were a number of battles in England between groups of the nobility. These unsettled times did not help England to prosper. The final battle of these 'Wars of the Roses' was the Battle of Bosworth Field (1485), when Henry Tudor, a Lancastrian, defeated Richard III, a Yorkist, and became king. Henry married Elizabeth of York and the Tudor rose, incorporating the red rose of Lancaster and the white rose of York, became the emblem of the age. The lasting peace between the groups of nobility allowed England to prosper and some people to become very rich. At the same time as wool became a major export, more land was given over to the rearing of sheep and people whose families had farmed the land for generations were evicted and became very poor.

Studying the Tudors provides an opportunity to develop children's historical skills, particularly in understanding the range of sources of information available and making inferences from evidence. There are opportunities for cross-curricular work particularly in literacy, mathematics and design and technology. In this activity section there are suggestions to support children's work in ICT.

SUGGESTED FURTHER ACTIVITIES

Pages 4 – 5 Tudor times
Take some photographs of the children at home or in class. Print them and ask the children what they were doing and thinking before the pictures were taken. Ask them to look at the pictures of Tudors in this book and ask them to imagine what the people in the pictures might have been doing or thinking before the pictures were made.

Pages 6 – 7 Landowners
The children could compare the costumes of a Tudor man and woman with those of a Victorian man and woman in a game at the following website: http://www.bbc.co.uk/history/society_culture/society/launch_gms_costumes.shtml.

Children could look at the family tree of the Howards, one of the richest families in Tudor times: http://tudors.crispen.org/howard_tree/index.html. Let them look for titles such as Duke, Duchess, Earl and Baron. See how many people in the tree lived before the beginning of Tudor times (1485) and trace the tree down to Katherine, who married Henry VIII.

Pages 8 – 9 Merchants
The children can find out a great deal about Tudor trade by visiting http://www.tudorbritain.org/trade/index.asp.

The answers to the 'Can you work it out?' questions are: (a) Two shillings and two pence, (b) two pounds and eleven shillings. The total is ten shillings and three pence.

Pages 10 – 11 Craftsmen and traders
When a journeyman wished to become a member of a craft guild, not only had he (or she) to pay money to the guild; it was also essential to make a piece of outstanding work – a masterpiece. Ask the children to make a masterpiece. It may be an item made in a craft lesson such as a piece of pottery or needlework. It could be bread or a cake, or sign writing. It should be something that the child has to work on and perhaps repeat until they feel that they have done their best. They could decide if their work is worthy of letting them join a guild.

The answers to the questions about the coats of arms are: (25) Saddlers – there are saddles on the shield, (26) Carpenters – there are pairs of compasses used for measuring on the shield, (38) Bowyers – there are bows above the shield.

Pages 12 – 13 Farming the land
Scroll down the following website with the children: http://www.applebymagna.org.uk/appleby_history/tudor_parish.htm. They can see the farming occupations of the people in the village of Appleby in late Tudor times.
If you scroll down further, the children can look at nine inventories.

Pages 14 – 15 The poorest people
Ask the children to use some of the following vagabond words (and those on page 15) in a sentence, as if they were a rogue or vagabond:

beak = Justice of the Peace	bung = a purse
chats = gallows	foist = pickpocket
glaziers = eyes	lift = to steal from a shop
prance = a horse	prig = to steal
snap = share of stolen goods.	

The sentence in the 'Vagabond talk' activity means: 'There are lots of people in the market for pickpockets to rob. Bring your stolen goods to the inn and we will get some food.'

Pages 16 – 17 Great houses

The children could make their own coat of arms. The essential features are the shield, the crest above it (which often features a helmet), and two supporters of the shield (sometimes lions, bears or birds). The coat of arms should reflect the child's interests.

Pages 18 – 19 Visiting a great house

The children could have a Tudor meal. A quite wealthy Tudor would have slices of cooked meats and chicken legs, a salad of lettuce, radish, cress and cucumber, a flat white bread roll, hard cheese, peaches, apricots and apple pie. A poor Tudor would have vegetable soup and bread.

The answer to the riddle is: A man (two legs) sits on a stool (three legs) with a leg of mutton (one leg) in his lap. A dog comes in (four legs) and runs off with the leg of mutton. The man picks up the stool, throws it at the dog and the dog brings the mutton back.

A more detailed investigation of great houses can be made at:
- http://www.cressbrook.co.uk/bakewell/chatswth.htm. Children can click on a slide show and a video showing a 360 degree panorama of the house to appreciate its size and grandeur.
- http://www.cressbrook.co.uk/bakewell/haddon.htm. This website also has a slide show of views outside and inside the house.
- http://renaissance.dm.net/compendium/52.html. This has a list of servants in a Tudor great house.
- http://renaissance.dm.net/com pendium/66.html and http://renaissance.dm.net/compendium/69.html. A steward's duties.
- http://renaissance.dm.net/compendium/51.html. This shows the wages earned by some of the staff at a great house.
- http://renaissance.dm.net/compendium/18.html. Children should scroll down to find the plants used to make homes smell pleasant. Many of these are available at garden centres and you may like the children to set up a Tudor herb garden, to extend their work.

Pages 20 – 21 Timber-framed houses

In Tudor times there was no standard spelling. Let the children write to each other, spelling as they like. Their letters should look as if they were written in Tudor times, but how easy are they to read?

The inventory items are:

Bedstead and bedding	35 s	10 d
Candle sticks	6s	9d
Pewter cups	3s	10d
Settle (bench with arms and back)	15s	6d
Pots and pans	2s	4d
Four lambs	5s	0d
Three sheep	12s	6d
Bacon and beef	2s	10d
Total	£4 4s	7d

Pages 22 – 23 Homes of the poor

Ask the children to make an inventory of a poor person's home, using the information on this double page to help them.

The lines of 'Ring a ring o' roses' are said to describe:
A rash of red circles forms on the skin.
Carrying a posy will protect against the plague.
Someone is sneezing.
We all die.

Pages 24 – 25 Helping the poor

The children should click on 'Tudor life' on the home page of http://www.tudorbritain.org/ and try the quiz.

Pages 26 – 27 Life in Tudor times

From the home page of http://www.tudorbritain.org/ the children should click on 'fun' to find out how the Tudors enjoyed themselves.

The children may like to compare life in their town with the following information about life in a Tudor town. Everyone is asleep through the night. Servants get up at 4.00 am. The church bells ring at 5.00 am for an early morning service. Shops open at 6.00 am. Everyone is at work or school by 7.00 am. Schools finish at 5.00 pm. Shops close at 7.00 pm.

ADDITIONAL RESOURCES

Websites

http://www.windowsonwarwickshire.org.uk/spotlights/rich_or_poor/tedderbiog2.htm   (Interactive website comparing rich and poor Tudors)

http://www.wealddown.co.uk/weald.htm   (Click on 'Bayleaf farmstead' to make a virtual tour of a timber-framed house.)

Books

A Tudor Journey by Philip Steele (Hodder Wayland) provides an illustrated account of a journey through Tudor England.

British History Makers series (Evans) includes books on the lives and times of *William Shakespeare* and *King Henry VIII*.

Daily Life in a Tudor House by Laura Wilson (Hamlyn) describes the life and home of a yeoman farmer and his family.

History through Poetry – Tudors by Neil Tonge (Hodder Children's Books) shows how poetry in Tudor times can be interpreted.

Tudor Children by Jane Shuter (Heinemann) describes Tudor times from a child's perspective.

Tudor Home by Alan Childs (Hodder Wayland) provides a wealth of information on the external and internal features of Tudor homes.

Rich and poor in Tudor times (Atlantic Europe Co Ltd) has a student book and teacher's guide supported by a picture poster pack and integrated website (available at www.CurriculumVisions.com).

Why did Henry VIII marry six times? by John Gorman (Evans) is designed for use with Unit 7 of the QCA History Scheme of Work.

Index